Soul Over Lightning

RAY GONZALEZ

THE UNIVERSITY OF
ARIZONA PRESS

TUCSON

The University of Arizona Press
www.uapress.arizona.edu

© 2014 Ray Gonzalez
All rights reserved. Published 2014

Printed in the United States of America
19 18 17 16 15 14   6 5 4 3 2 1

Cover design by Leigh McDonald
Cover photo by Mark Byzewski

Publication of this book was made possible in part by proceeds of a permanent
endowment created with the assistance of a Challenge Grant from the National
Endowment for the Humanities, a federal agency.

Library of Congress Cataloging-in-Publication Data
González, Ray.
  [Poems. Selections]
  Soul Over Lightning : poems / Ray González.
      pages cm. — (Camino del Sol: a Latina and Latino Literary Series)
   ISBN 978-0-8165-3100-4 (pbk. : alk. paper)
  1. Southwest, New—Poetry. 2. Mexican-American Border Region—Poetry. I. Title.
  PS3557.O476A6 2014
  811'.54—dc23
                                   2013045541

♾ This paper meets the requirements of ANSI/NISO Z39.48-1992 (Permanence of
Paper).

Contents

—PART THREE—

Acknowledgments

I would like to thank the editors for previously publishing some of the poems in the following journals:

American Poetry Review: "The Owl"
Anti: "Dark Star"
Best American Poetry 2003: "Max Jacob's Shoes"
Bitter Oleander: "Beautiful," "Defend the Day," and "Memory House"
Caliban: "Balata," "Eyes of a Saint," and "Rufino Tamayo"
Conduit: "I Stepped on the Head of Man Ray"
Malpais Review: "West of West"
MiPOesias: "The Miracle"
New American Writing: "He Calls His Dog Rimbaud"
Puerto del Sol: "The White Hair"
The Writing Disorder: "A Made Place That Is Mine"

I would like to thank the University of Minnesota's Faculty Imagine Fund and its Scholar of the College Fellowship Program, along with the Vermont Studio Center, for support and space to complete many of these poems. I wrote many of them in the memory of my late friend, Morton Marcus, and of my late teacher and mentor, Robert Burlingame. This book is dedicated to them. With friendship and respect for their poetry, I thank George Kalamaras, John Bradley, Phil Woods, and Juan Felipe Herrera.

Soul Over Lightning

—PART ONE—

I Slept in a Cave

I slept in a cave and did not
know where I was, why it
was important to see the light
return to show me the exit.
I slept in a cave and saw
a fire in the heart, how it
flickered away.
I slept in a cave of dripping
walls and listened to the water
escape toward the entrance
of my dream where the faces
of animals covered the bleeding
ground, men running away
without taking what they
had spilled before me,
the herds of yesterday becoming
the angry hordes of tomorrow.
I slept in a cave and learned
to trace its walls with a will
that remained invisible, yet
brought me closer to scraping
my soul against the rocks to
find I had always slept there.

I tried to wake when I rolled
closer to the paintings, saw
things I can't describe because
my closed eyes had already
seen what took place, how
things were created underneath
and not from above because
many men slept up there,
away from creation and what
it sheltered inside the mountain.
I slept in a cave and grew into

an old man wise with eyesight
and dumb with my hands,
a blind man wanting to feel
his way out of the dark tunnel
that his mother opened when
she screamed upon his birth.

The Bird

The bird that lands in the sun
is your child asking for you

to find stars she can burn
on her lips.

The bird that lands in the willow tree
is your secret coming apart,

its wings teaching you how to survive
after the piano stopped playing

and the guitar kept smoking
beyond the revolution.

The bird that disappears in the mirror
is someone you knew long ago,

his touch the dance of the stranger
who showed you the way to the mountain.

The bird nestled in your hand is your way
of speaking, the smell of its feathers

the hush of the dove that
gently alights in your palm.

Du Fu in Early Winter

My old poetry teacher is dead
and my wife plays her violin upstairs.
When I sit in the basement,
I pretend I walk across the desert,
my teacher appearing on the other
side of the rocks to show me
the pictographs move if you look.
I listen to the violin wail in a way
no poem can.

My teacher once read me a poem
by Du Fu and I imagined standing
on the bridge with the old Chinese
poet and thinking "I am here."
His poem revealed the hands of
the flowers and the mist of love
that Du Fu had for the moon.

My old poetry teacher is dead
and my wife repeats her tune,
getting it right as the notes
cross the house and echo from
the closed windows because,
outside, the first snow is falling
for Du Fu again.

Vertigo

I see the atrium of the world
as it spins in my vision, wondering
if weeks of vertigo means the axis
of my eyes is warped for good.
When I think of Du Fu at the gates
of the emperor, my head spins
and my doctor wants to know
what a poem is for as he checks
my inner balance.
I try to cross the room and can't
without hugging tables and chairs
as if the inner earthquake is shaking
my tongue and eyes, making sure
I never remember my lyrics.

When I see William Butler Yeats
spinning in the flowers, I am
mistaken for a drunk fool
who can't see straight.
I don't share that image with
anyone because the branches
of winter are bare and their black
lines lead to the back of my head
where something is wrong,
a signal for Du Fu to begin
his journey home.

I see the instruments of slaughter
are still in the news and hope
the new year allows me to see
how peace is a dream that vertigo
mixes with a lie or two.
When I rose this morning,
it was 24 degrees below zero
and the world was quiet.
When I got up, I was not dizzy
and memorized a poem or two.

Comfort

When I stand next to the barrel cactus,
its flowers are tiny red stars of wisdom
showing me the dry path.

When I kneel in the dirt and can't
cut into the green for water, my thirst
is for the territory I left behind.

Sometimes when I go back
and find the cottonwood by the river,
its burned black trunk waits for the sun

to set and the fire to be gone.
I know its soul is not afraid to leave
as I climb into the valley and move

aside to let low clouds drift by.
When the air clears, it is the season
of the white lizards I was warned about.

The Road

When the coyote appeared on
the road, I should have slowed
down so we could stare at
each other, the animal frozen
in the headlights, its eyes ablaze,
the pinpoint line from eye to
eye marking the first moment
I arrived no longer afraid.
I looked in the rearview mirror
and it was gone, a white blur
crossing behind me.

I returned to kiss the desert as
if landscape was going to save me,
those distant brown peaks looking
the same, decade after decade,
though the road now goes through
them and turns back onto itself
before the river takes it home.
Even the cottonwoods are alone
and spread their arms over water
that wants to take them, too.

Twilight burns beyond their branches,
the thorn in my foot pulled by men
on horses centuries ago because
the one who drives home is the one
who prefers to walk alone.
I recognized the approaching canyon
as the opening in the earth where
God forgot to breathe, his massive
weight changing the mountain into
steps for ascending the stars, though
the light in the middle of the vast
Chihuahua is not for salvation,
but finding a way through, even
if the road passes and I stop
where the mountains rise.

The Miracle

Striking his head and falling,
reaching and scraping the snakes
on the way down.
Drowning, weaving and straining,
moving down the canyon,
escaping to be caught, landing
and igniting after many whispers,
burning with what could not be

rewritten, landing into place,
standing upright, out of breath
gone from the circle that granted
him ability, stiff and tall as he
illustrates the wall with his body,
arms extended like a worn cross
left behind when he fell, his long

white hair on fire now, the smoke
branding the room with the smell
of his changing face, the shadow
taking its place behind him as he
breathes and opens his eyes,
a mark on his chest where his
heart fell ahead of him, the room
covered in flowers, vines growing
around his legs, tying him down
in thorns, saved to be taught,
held against the wall by those

to be studied and accused,
seeing him inside their thoughts
when they take him apart,
the prize paid to gaze upon him
paid before his fall, their realization
his body is trembling, the silence

charging the room with the truth
of arrows, knives, clusters of stars,
bones embedded in animals, brains
cooked in clay ovens as they pray
together, rosaries decorating
muscles and thighs that sweat with
dirt given and soil taken away,

blood cakes eaten before he moves
again and forms ropes on his wrists
that burn to be broken, the fire in his
hair spreading to preserve him,
the blossoming smell of excavation
digging around him, trying to move
the dirt wall so his silhouette smolders
into blackness rubbed on foreheads

chanting that something will happen,
the words stirring his blackened face,
the sting opening his eyes, scorpion
memory marking the wall over his
broken shoulders, belief crushing
his feet, openings in the earth defined
by the smoke that covers the others.

Drawing the Owl

One of the first things
I did upon my release from
the hospital was draw a picture
of an owl in my notebook,
a distorted bird staring at
the space between the mind
and severe depression,
the mighty force of its eyes
making me sketch carefully,
though crookedly. The owl stood
on the branch until I recovered,
its ruffled brown head and
folded wings bracing for
what comes after healing.
I add a tiny mark on the drawing
each time the owl flies and
a mark when it returns,

the bird portraying what can't
be found, the only real owl
I ever saw lifting its huge gray
wings from the tree next to
a decaying cabin in a field
of Montana, its sudden rising
draping it across my car's
windshield for an instant,
a presence called back because
it was too early for its flight.

Notebook

Smoke drifts like words
you used to know.

The act between seeing
and believing twists

the huge white moth.
When you go barefoot,

no one can follow
where you went.

Belief is the object outside
itself, radioactive cows

running past a shattered
Japanese nuclear reactor,

the herd stampeding
the reporter on the news.

Trains pass the insane
asylum every day and

baboons recognize
words on a computer.

The sentence is inside
the period, though it is

too late for the departure of
the fabulous fishing Virgin

because she is immaculate.

Several Beliefs

1

The weather is cold and dark.
No one knows if animals dream.
Men go to the source once too often.

Shame covers them in hooker beads
and tattoos of someone they once loved.
How does the weather fit in?

Storms do not allow moonlight,
though the young men walk like birds.
No one expected them to act this way.

The clouds are our ancestors,
lost and floating in prayer.
No one calls it resurrection.

The weather is rich and satisfied.
After the snowfall, artifacts are found
to prove, once, there was a village here.

2

The law of the closed fist
is to open the hand.

When it rains, the old man
finishes his cup of tea.

The song is over
and his feet hurt.

He sits waiting for
the dark face of the plant

in the vase to show him
what has been.

The law of the wrinkled
finger is to point with one.

He finally stands and welcomes
the autumn calm, his hands

at his side, the things he didn't
see waiting for him outside.

3

The red-tailed hawk flew out
of the backyard tree.

It was huge and startled me.
What is the word for an instant

shadow crossing the horizon?
What did I see? When we look,

each shape returns to warn us
we are too deep into the trees.

4

When the moon strikes twelve,
the blessed Virgin guards the cross
with the figure smoking up there,
arms extended.
Heaven arrives and heaven leaves,
each sermon ringing as if
someone is descending.

Have you ever counted
your heirloom rosary beads

as you fingered them,
not for grief but for answers?
Not for the red beads pressed
from Spanish roses of the body,
their scent alive after eighty years.

Not for mystery, but finding
the necklace is holy when held to
the light, a manner of gathering
flowers instead of stones.

5

There were clay bodies everywhere,
the soul over lightning.
The dark star was never played again.
Twilight was involved, though
penumbra refused.

Muddy hands were outlawed,
water and sand composing it.
There was a steeple.
A light existed.
Walls were strong and painted
and hallways led to nowhere.

Men rose and fell.
Long hair grew down their backs.
Women fed and women were granted.
Roses grew and roses left thorns.
There were clay bodies everywhere.
Windows opened and never closed.
Imagine wings and gates.
Damaged spines spit out hallucinations.

There were clay feet.
No one moved.
Knees were bent in the circle of rock.
They were able to imagine fire.

The clay bowl discovered itself
and carnal scenes were emblazoned.
A flight of roots became a cough
and they listened.

Clay hands built the text.
Cracks in the sun, in the brick.
There are ruins at rest.
Dig there.
The body that opens its hands first
will extend the life lines on its palms.

6

I look for a book that destroys
itself after one reading, its shadow
mouthing words not in the text.

"Good form is the value of a lie,"
Mina Loy said, but the human
body comes out of the flower.

One man asks for a flame
while another demands
the thought, not the sentence.

We can't know where we are
because the prayer stick of
the Zunis is encased in glass,

its faded colors making sense.
I don't know its words that
could save me because the book

of the judge cast me inside
the mountain, a broken treaty
burying my name there.

Strength at Aguirre Springs, New Mexico

The image of your face
is hard to trace because

the sun hits the clouds
the instant you turn to

the glow in the trees
and realize the light is

behind you as you hold
onto the wind's majesty—

not impossible to miss
if you climbed this far.

The urge for revenge is
hidden in the oak's heart,

though the camera does
not capture the moment

that swallows each foot
of grass, your mind at

sunset shaping toward
the window that never

closes, a quiet image
invisible to the touch,

your presence resolved in
the shaking of the leaves,

camera on your face that
is too dark to move,

dust floating from the tree
to cover you with a layer

outlining the seconds as
you open your eyes

to study the oak because
the click of the camera

pulls you into the bark
where its wrinkles hold you,

something approaching
on the horizon, the first

lightning bolt igniting
the mind into silence,

the stone steps leading
to broken ground where

rain moves on your skin.

The White Hair

The apparition of a white hair at the bottom of my glass appeared to me to be a good omen. I felt ideas and ideas being born and vanishing . . . . "This is my first white hair!" . . . This . . . was the "elixir of long life."

—SALVADOR DALI

The white hair appears as a sign
to another life and you are living it.
The hair is the musical note of destiny,
white line between desire and fulfillment,
the border between having what you want
and reconstructing the shadow of what
you cannot possess.

The white hair at the bottom of the clay jar
was dropped by an old woman who used
to love you, but is now shedding longer hair
in the cups of men who do not want her.
Did she drop it as a warning?

The hair traces the opening to heaven,
makes you balder as it fills your jar with
things you do not know.
The white hair of a long life belongs to
someone who whispers, "Come to me.
I am here."

Yet, the white hair you abruptly notice
hanging off your lips is a nuisance
you pull off with a shrug as you drink from
your jar and let go, the white hair disappearing
as it hits the floor.

The Secret Book of Sand

In the secret book of sand, it is written,
"The son who returns is the son in command."

I returned and Cottonwood Springs burned
atop the Franklin Mountains.

In the secret book, it is said,
"The guilty son is the son in demand."

I fed myself lechuga and cactus greens with
sweat from the clouds keeping guilt away.

In the book, it is thought,
"The son with a book learns its sentences

are written with grains of sand."
I came back with chapters to be written.

In the secret book, it is proclaimed,
"The son who arrives celebrates

because his hands are cleansed with
the blank pages, at last."

Amarma

The night's eye in the foliage of famine.
The bristling fox in the tattered trees.
The graves of children burned in a fire.
The change of advisors leading their souls astray.
The closeness of a triangle and a tooth.
The system of radishes vanishing again.
Their blind roots transforming rage.
The sessions from another era changing the landscape.
The imitation of arrow and sharp spleen.
The coat and hat left behind the stairs.
The pebbles by the river useless and untouched.
The notes of skeletal history collected to please.
The night's eye in the dance of mushrooms.
The speaking owl hidden in the hands.
The water moving around the green logs.
The stolen glance shaping all things.
The flame growing on a knot in the tree.
The cluster of bathed demons breathing in balance.
The sudden door closed and locked.
The flimsiest of reasons saving the neighborhoods.
The clouds moving into the distant valley.
The phrase lying in doubt before rapture arrives.
The gate to the bridge falling into the river.
The game room simply a family album.
The night's eye blinking for the last time.
The music from the lower spheres heard too soon.
The prelude about the night the moon fell.

For the Convenience of the Reader

For the convenience of the reader,
it will not snow again for 47 years.
Eight seagulls will land on the pier,
hovering until the hurricane makes
it essential to remove the last chapter.
The reader will wonder what happened,
how unfair it is to end without
revealing who came the closest
to loving another person.
For the convenience of the reader,
something will be missing because
the surrender to God was not
part of the text.

For the sake of the witness,
the text will lead to a more
powerful conclusion where things
get resolved by a couple walking
along the pier in search of words
they have not shared in years.
The reader will feel comfortable
and the creator will open a drawer
and finger the rosary his mother
gave him on her death bed.

—PART TWO—

West of West

1

If you hold your hands together at San Cristobal,
the cliff edge will bless you and you can see the sun
between your fingers, its fire dimming west of west,
behind your pounding heart that descended
from the Oro Mountains on time.
In his journals across the deserts of Texas,
Cabeza de Baca met the people and wrote how
they had to weep for half an hour before speaking,
this custom keeping him alive, the visitor from
the broken sky shedding his naked skin twice
a year, writing how he left parts of himself behind,
his body peeling in the sun that burned west of
his hands and near the hungry people that
refused to eat until their hunters returned.
Once, Cabeza extracted a huge arrowhead from
the chest of a wounded warrior, showing his
people how to stitch the wound, the man
recovering while the people took the arrowhead
and ran from village to village, pronouncing
they found a healer, exhibiting the arrowhead
for years after the stranger left.

2

You are inside the mountain and can't breathe.
The ice and darkness resemble Senecú del Sur,
eroding walls of dirt south of your hands and
west of your sweating head, ropes tying your
wrists to the stone table, whispers growing closer,
the sound of water singing as if the great rooms
will finally open and you can see what happened
to the family after the railroads came, how your
grandfather worked the line, then disappeared

among the Apaches of southern Arizona,
the lone witness to their creation myth where
the battle of the beasts takes place across
the Sonora, his version of the story bringing
you the first words you set down on paper.

3

If you walk the Rio Grande southeast of El Paso,
you might come upon the site where the starving
Cabeza and his black companion, Estebanico,
met two Indian women after seven years of
wandering the desert. The two men were fed
and disappeared again, heading south where
your hands mark the soil with a finger or
a knife, even with Spanish words forbidden by
the people who knew the strangers were the gods
the elders dreamed about, the vision of
the mountain and the highest tree turning
into a fire far from what the women believed.
You can hike along the now dangerous miles,
the other side of the border waiting with guns,
masked men, and something left unwritten
by Cabeza. You can pause and pretend there
is a stone marker there though, what would it say?

4

Near the Rio Sonora, stands a tree,
the only remaining evidence of the Town
of Hearts where the people gave Cabeza
600 opened deer hearts. He wrote they hunted
them in abundance and had plenty to eat,
the hearts a gift needed to keep moving west,
the threatening mountains turning purple
in the wanderer's hands, the tree surviving
the centuries because it is a *mago*—a poisonous

tree whose fruit the people picked to dip
their arrows into the juice, the poison
appearing as milk if there was no fruit,
deer that licked the tree dropping dead,
their small bodies turning to stone in
the desert sun, Cabeza carrying the deer
hearts across time because the leaves of
the tree left marks on his hands—dark spots
that resembled a map he studied before
the sun disappeared each night and his
arms throbbed with the weight of faith.

5

West of the mountains, Pedro Robledo died,
the young conquistador falling ill after
the expedition crossed one hundred miles
of desert in the 110 degree heat, Don Juan
de Oñate driving the men on, promising
the river would appear again north of
the heat, his men thirsty and lost, some of
them suddenly excited when one of their
dogs returned with wet, muddy feet.
They followed it to the water that saved
them, Perillo Springs in the Jornada del
Muerto now a legend more than a place,
the exact spot they were saved by a dog
vanishing when the river was dammed,
the springs becoming a lake—the lake
spreading into heaven as heaven opened
into a cool, dark place in the middle
of nowhere.

6

You are inside the mountain, the terrible
awakening forcing them to cut the ropes,

sit you up and show you how the beasts
in the tale were armed with clubs, though
the eagle taught its tribe how to use bows
and arrows against the dragons that invaded
its nest, reptiles from the desert and snakes
from the sky. The Apache whispers bring
rattlesnakes and let you live among them,
though the enclosing circle of rattles
beats closer as if your hands were still tied,
the coiled earth climbing into your heart
to welcome you home, grant you the stone
table of those forced to believe by marching
across a place where they always belonged,
the serpent unable to be killed in the myth
where one giant rattler survived the battle
and hid in the cliff of a mountain in Arizona,
its eyes turning into brilliant stones that can
be seen to this day if you look west of your
captivity and near the road where the family
finally let go of their hands in the desert.

Eyes of a Saint

Eyes of a saint. The star.
Eyes of a lizard. The sound.
You can't decipher bread.

Eyes of a light bulb.
The way invented, painted red so skin
of the whale assumes its place in history.

Eyes of a saint. The car.
Eyes of a butterfly.
Involvement and eyes of a twig.

The road erased. The map replaced.
Eyes of a saint. The scar.

Corrupted artery, soft tongue, shaken tree.
Shaved head of the saint, shaved eyelash of his mother,
shaved chest of his father, shaved soul of his brother.

Shaved, no, saved soul leaking.
The entrance frame by frame.

The flame. Three species of inquisitor.
Eyes of a demon. Not fame but war.
Dead PTSD nephew.

Birds. Shoes. Folded man.
Eyes of a wooden leg. Eyes of a bent elbow.
Eyes under the bloody bandage.

Eyes assuming what is seen is not painted.
Eyes of a saint. Flawed telling.
Warped legend.
Prayer messages to the unborn.

Defend the Day

Snow in May and a return to a gray sky
where the dark train overlooks a child
taking shape, the faults of the indoor coast

as casual as the black rocks on the head
of the iguana, three rubber balls floating
in the sea, thieves pounding melodies on

wood because a voice is thinking, each
thought comparable to a man abandoning
his house with a solution, his eyelids as wet

as the flank of the last surviving horse,
the animal that floated down after faith
became a guessing game and the paperweight

on the desk grew tired, its gravity a dying rose
sent in time for the morning to release mud
from under the closed doors, this shift in

the earth having nothing to do with sorrow,
only the spreading notion that the river current
is embracing a piece of jade.

Gluing Photographs of the Petroglyphs Into My Scrapbook

In the state park, I photographed
ancient art on the stones, volcanic
slabs releasing arrows, birds,
and horses into the river.
The symbols were a brighter color
than the horses as if a message
was passed from rock to rock.
Stick figures danced in a circle
and the night brought fires that
never went out.

I Xeroxed my original photo
and cut petroglyphs into a
puzzle, my thoughts on the cliff
a burned text.
I re-arranged the cut-out symbols,
but the pattern I glued was not
my own and I tried to decipher
what I was shown when I climbed
to stare at the marked rocks.

I glued them into a scrapbook,
animals and arrows encircling
the hill above the river where
someone scraped the rocks so
they could speak.
I saw another visitor crouching
behind boulders where designs
painted the ground.
I waited but he never stood,
designs on the rocks fading
because my fingers needed time
to trace themselves into the past.

Staring at Rodin

The severed head of John the Baptist
lies in the glass, eyes of shock looking at

The Thinker whose massive feet are gnarled
against the rock of what you live through

when you see how Rodin mounted the body
against the blackness of the inescapable cord—

the fiber of the fused man and woman who twist
out of the same maze of bone, lovers leaving

their brains under the great weight of Rodin's hands.
There is a silence dying between these statues,

the planet of sculpture revolving around the loss
of Rodin—his secret emotion he accidently chipped

off an unsuccessful project we will never see, only
know his agony—the spring toward the air where

his cast hands were the same white forms that pulled
the earth from its sinking orbit, the fibers of rock

pressing down to change the history of one man,
one white surface, one touch of chisel escaping from

the sculpture of the flying head of John the Baptist.
Museums block the air of desire with these forms,

the agony of rock and heart becoming a music that
has no sound, no system—the severed head of John

the Baptist falling as the heaviest matter of faith.
The Thinker moves in the next century, his gigantic

feet consuming the smell of the earth so the frozen
love of fissures and the cracking stink of blown shards

can blacken for centuries. It is why Rodin forced
himself to mold and cut the long thin man with

the massive penis, the thin man standing naked
on the pedestal far from the land of The Thinker.

John the Baptist and his head fever across the room
from the thin man who is shocked so much belongs

here, encased in glass or jabbed into the controlled air
of display so the anguish of cutting his sins into one

moment of suspended entrails is all Rodin needed
to carve himself into the missing body of John the Baptist.

I Stepped on the Head of Man Ray

I stepped on the head of Man Ray
and my family portraits fell out.

I stepped on the head of Man Ray
and elderly health care oozed out.

When Man Ray said stop, I studied
picture after picture with my foot

holding his head down because
my photograph was in there.

In the cruelty of my long illness,
my healed mind left the hospital,

Man Ray's photo of robotic flowers
the map to the traitor who turned me

in and took Man Ray away to shoot
objects that never suffered.

I stepped on the head of Man Ray
and chemical development of photos

opened its long, sleek legs
to give me a peek or two.

I was not ready and waited for Man Ray
to get off the floor with a hard head,

stare at me, and reach for his camera.
In the steadiness of my recovery,

Man Ray took a picture of me, though
I have never seen it and there is a rumor

it lies in his archives—the shot when
I blinked and a certain light emerged.

The Face of the Beggar

The face of the beggar
in the cafe, the deep melon
in my wrist, a pause in my
meal as he stares, hunger
dripping from his lips.

The face of the beggar,
my full stomach in line
to pay, unfinished plate
left for him to steal.

The face of the beggar,
disbelief and a lyrical fall,
Charles Mingus playing his
stand-up bass and singing,
"Don't be afraid.
The clown is afraid, too."

Memory House

The adobe air in the lungs covers
the one who enter the ruins.

When he finds a pottery shard,
he forces himself to leave it there.

When he reaches the imploded room,
something moves near the wall

where the patterns drawn on
the bricks resemble a pair

of humans running away from
tomorrow, though they live in

the house of thought without
having to remember everything.

There is a secret corner safe
from centuries of footsteps.

Its memory is secluded in one
room without entering shadows.

When the last visitor wanders in
seven rooms, he emerges with closed

eyes and recalls the man who wrote
"rooms of poetry have no roofs"

because, to speak in the memory
house, is to recall what took place

in each room before leaving open
a crumbling doorway into the earth.

Dark Star

Above the moon, a lynx takes a maid.
How can this thought open the door

to the swollen river, a kissing mouth,
an avocado changing on the shelf?

How often have you counted your
toes before going to sleep?

The magnolia's golden leaves belong
to the traveler.

Night as a beautiful arrow.
Night as your cold fingers rewrite this

to include the entrance and the exit.
Is it true you are a broken sundial?

There is sacrifice inside the cottonwood,
but did you see the owl in the saguaro?

Origin

I watch the box elder beetle crawl
slowly across the window sill,

abandon origins when I write,
"The old man emerged from the lightning strike

and everything seemed eerily calm," then
realize someone has already written that.

My old poems about rattlesnakes sound composed
by someone who knows nothing about snakes.

The sidewalk is covered by tiny flowers growing
through the concrete, yellow petals rising

above the cracks to form delicate strings.
Home is lost in a language whose origin

was changed by people crossing the illegal border.
I wish I knew the origin of the word "indicial" when

box elder beetles disappear into the wall of the house
and there is no river left to cross.

A Made Place That Is Mine

after Robert Duncan

The yellow field turns
thought into a cottonwood

that shaded me as a boy.
If a sentence holds memory,

why do I erase these words?
After they disappear,

they make me a stranger learning
what I thought I already knew.

The birth of my mother is
mightier than this sentence.

Not the sentence,
but the thought under the tree.

They

The tiny, yellow bird slammed
into the glass door, fluttered

on the ground and died.
She buried it and the bird landed

on its legs when she dropped
it in the hole, a shovelful of dirt

changing everything, the young
soldier holding the shovel

because his hands were a nest,
no one in the family resembling

the young soldier.
He died alone.

No one erases lines from old notebooks.
They turn yellow on their own.

Cesar Vallejo and the Mule

When Cesar Vallejo faced the mule, the starving animal kicked dust into the air and brayed with a music that gave the poet an idea. The mule ran in circles inside the fence and Vallejo stared, his eyebrows bent by shadows he couldn't see, dark movements at his back reminding him there were starving women looking for him. His words, based on an idea from a stubborn mule, formed on his lips as a cough, the thunder in the sky making him open the gate and face the animal. The mule stopped, head to the ground, as Vallejo entered and raised his arms. Old men in the hills heard a cry and thought it was a sign from heaven. When they came down into the valley, the soil they worked became the dirt of the poet.

By the time they reached the fence and searched the empty hut, there was no Vallejo to be found. A poem had been dropped in the hay, but the old men turned their backs on poetry long ago. The lone sheet of paper contained Vallejo's last poem. The old men didn't know that when Cesar faced the mule, the hungry beast took his arm off with its mighty jaws. It ran across the plowed fields with Cesar's arm in its mouth. The animal was eventually caught by the old men and brought back to the corral, the arm not spoken about as it was tossed into the fire pit. When the mule rested in its pen, the sheet of paper in the hay wrinkled in the sun, its blood reading, "This is where I am going, this is where I have been."

South Past Albuquerque, Guided by Rain

Everyone in the car was afraid,
yet we talked about it.

The men came in the night,
then went away in black rain.

It was the empty road to San Miguel,
the curve toward La Union,

the moon forgotten on the road because
it was the path to Kilbourne Hole.

Everyone had a story to tell.
Some got told, some were changed

to keep families alive.
One man spoke about the eagle

that descended at Cuchillo,
bending the tree with its weight,

then flying away with a small
bundle in its claws, the fear

everyone worshipped returning when
the eagle dropped white stones.

We talked about the bird as
we drove south past Albuquerque

guided by the quiet rain.
When it stopped, the road glistened

with the sweat of the storyteller
who is never afraid.

The Distance Between Two Rooms

Walls and the creation of the world * enhanced interior * everyone so
serious * jewels thrown at her feet * a window composed of yesterday *
a large corridor vacuumed in time to lie down * suffering superstitions *
synthesis and canned goods * white walls of the hospital * seasons providing
for the furniture * human affairs * pure water * good room over his head
* immaculate reconstruction * sharp nails through the floor * rat poison
* embers and cold fish * brooms to sweep hair under the rug * nocturnal
wishes* diamond necklaces * earwax and spit * unframed pictures * framed
masterpieces * windows without glass * curtains without windows * good
hallway over his head * true voyagers * doorknobs encased in honey *
mansions * apartments * bungalows * rooms so small they smell * water
and bread * legs of dark clouds * the distance between two thoughts in
the hospital * the distance between the chair and the closet * the distance
between the room and itself * the distance between two places * a cockroach
inside the room * a very clean room * a circular adjective * brains * pianos *
ice cubes * rubber bands * origami mistakes * folded rags and mops waiting
to clean the patient's room * one chair * two lamps * one table * one bed *
two rooms finally two rooms * strings of worry * strings of dirt * cobwebs
* strings of soap * the distance between can't say it * the distance between
* the distance * the house not a house but a situation * construction halted
* property * awarded flowers * painted flowers * locks inserted * walls
smashed * the cost of living * the celebration * trim lawns * a pattern on
paper where geometric hunger is fed with an alloy calculated from an iron
compound extracted from the chest of Ezra Pound though state hospitals
and incarceration have nothing to do with the distance breathed beyond the
years of calling.

The Second Miracle

Waking, crawling, entering,
assuming the horses are loose,
suggesting, burrowing, rising to love
the horizon that bends into the mountain,
he dries himself in the sand, watching,
recalling how he merged under the barbed
wire, caught, returned, detained, caught
again before the river fell in, swimming,
gasping, involving, witnessing the deep
sand figures come alive, twisted in sunken
wire exposed to the currents, foaming
in surprise, carrying him past the boundary,
throwing him, flying him, forgetting him
as he lies on the bank, afraid but not
fearful, several bodies melting into
the ground, shoes and shirts drying
into tomorrow's population evading
the water to learn the alphabet of mud
that drips out of their ears, his head
mistaken for a fossil thrown up after
too many drowned, his memory
leaving marks, the dark thing following
him, praying for him as it gets closer,
his sudden rising as magnificent as
the red stain of the sun leaving the sky,
his feet sinking in his father's mud,
the old man's arms and legs sticking
out of the cotton field to warn him
the house of his father is not
the home of his son.

The Ghost at San Elizario, Texas

The shadow moves inside the old
adobe jail, swirls into the wall
and disappears in front of me.
Who died here and who got away?
The ancient cells are locked, their
dirt floors below ground.
I saw someone in there when
I walked up to read the historic marker.
The shape scratched the wall
with names of those who were
imprisoned to hold the walls up.

I walk around the small building,
whispers hissing below my feet,
buried movement down there,
though the dead prisoners escaped
through the roof, bodies flying above
the cottonwoods, the broken beams
mistaken for the hanging tree.

I hear the rattling chains, the song
ringing through centuries of mud,
my careful circling noticed by two
Mexican men across the dirt lot,
one of them shaking his head at me,
the other pointing to the road,
warning me to move along because
he has been inside and seen.

Is This It?

The wars continue and the snowman in the backyard has not melted in three months of bitter cold. My 23-year-old nephew lies in a veteran's grave as his story appears in the *New York Times*, an article about overmedicated veterans returning to a country that ignores them. History will not change, but photos of my family stare at me from the newspaper. These five foot walls of snow surround everything and the curtain falls on public protest. A starving rabbit runs across the snow. I put the newspaper down and watch the animal through the window, looking for the details as its frozen tracks turn the careful snowflakes to ice and start the next blizzard toward a white out where the blinding light means all wars begin at home.

Blame

Blame the beetle that eats the tree to kill it
with color and a disease that rearranges
the vast landscape until it travels too far
on hungry wings that turn brittle and fall off,
floating into the left eye of someone with
no name, no secrets or religions searching
for him so he can stop writing the text.

Blame the sidewinder for leaving marks
on the white sand, though white sand was
outlawed by those who do not believe in
the blind road that circles until Trinity is
set off again across the desert hills whose
radioactive pieces of blue glass are teardrops
of scientists who made too many mistakes.

Blame the weather for hiding what is out
there and what is hidden in the belly button
where no one touches the inside of the bell,
an innocent child learning how to come forth
into the violent world.

Family of Water

Family of water outside the forgotten storm. Family of water beside the
running stream. Family of water above the recited oath. Family of water
below the hidden earth. Family of water where someone stepped long ago.
Family of water where a ghost is forbidden to dwell. Family of water ahead
of the sweating forehead. Family of water behind the afterglow. Family
of water ignored on the map. Family of water discovered in the second
world. Family of water deep in the eyebrow. Family of water shallow in the
brain. Family of water frozen in the arms. Family of water exploding in
the chest. Family of water echoing out of the cave. Family of water buried
in denial. Family of water outlining the coast. Family of water erasing the
shore. Family of water worn like a footstep. Family of water skipped in the
fog. Family of water eaten at the table. Family of water thirsting for more.
Family of water covered in blankets. Family of water denying the sun is
exposed. Family of water whispering as foam. Family of water flooding the
tongue. Family of water evaporating thought. Family of water shrunk to a
black mole on the shoulder.

At the Time of the Armistice

The sleeping children woke up and their sad mothers quit weeping. Men whispered among themselves as if something was not properly decided, even if their side created the earthquake and the other side invented the first typewriter. The treaty was improperly signed, though the circus tent was left open for 24 hours, the horizon filled with restless coffins of 23 year olds who came back with numerical legends tattooed on their shattered foreheads. The sleeping children woke to the sound of bristling wings and couldn't believe the day's lesson in school involved taking crayons out of their boxes to color funny faces of people they didn't know. When the giggling and wonder died down, the children held their colored pages in the air and their mothers wept.

Joseph Cornell's Diary Entry One Day After I Was Born, September 21, 1952

Dream of color objects
Strange toys
Stars clear

—PART THREE—

After Reading Octavio Paz

He wants to enter the adobe wall,
disappear into it and dissolve into
the mud as if spirit is dry earth
and the ground is the heart
where everyone was born with
a mark on their foreheads.
He wants to stay inside the wall
until the sun burns a deep color
into his trapped though open hands,
the wave of heat making his hair
stand on end like black snakes that
slithered into the wall to reinforce
what was built, a fountain of dust
raining in the grand room, clouding
over midnight cries and whispers,
the groans and sighs of lost origins
where he used to love.

He is alive between the beams,
the cracked bricks the crumbs
of a god and his meal, the mind
that meets architectural silence
as the corridor of time explodes
into grains of fine sand on his
arms so he can extend the wall
up into the clouds, each thought
opening and shutting the lone
window because the tree outside
walks into the room and spreads
its branches until the four walls
are touched, its reign of green
pushing space apart, his battle
to grasp what the wall desires,
how faster the mud breathes
each time he wants to emerge
and run outside.

The Clay Jars

The potter shaped two breasts on each flesh
colored jar, the round objects resembling short
women with no heads, two breasts on each jar.

Set in a group, they are headless mothers begging
the world to quit taking their sons. Seven of
them have short arms extended to the sky.
The other two are different.

One is set on its arms, its legs in the air,
like a woman standing on her hands.
There is no head, stunted arms supporting
the pot as if she is completing a cartwheel.
Why does she seem so happy with no head,
while the others weep for their sons?

The ninth pot is a headless, breasted woman
bending over on her knees, the hole in back
showing what looks like the handle to
the broom she uses to sweep the floor.

This is not a violation because all nine pots
have broomsticks sticking out of each,
breasts proud and defiant as something
seeps out, women radiating moisture from
within, bringing tears, perhaps milk,
to overflowing at the top.

The Mathematics of Ecstasy

The huge panel borders the edge of the galaxy,
though the dark man at the bottom right of
the painting seems confused as if the star
cluster to his left is a white fist coming at him.

The colors of Eden are swirling out of
the immense white matter weaving at the top,
while two planets bounce off each other
without taking the dark man, fragments of
memory cascading in space because

the ecstatic moment must be earned as
the circular, black shape at the top searches
for a partner. If this is true, the dark man
changes in creation because the sun has
become extinct, the artist using it to construct

equations about the distorted, dark man
who is moving his enormous head because
the galaxy has been solved as he dreams
there are walls of stars he has yet to see.

Max Jacob's Shoes

They were found after his death
by someone who needed shoes.
When this man plucked them
out of a mountain of trash,
Max Jacob's shoes came alive.
They fit this person as if truth
had never left and he slowly
walked away from the filth.
It took him days to realize
he wore the shoes of a poet.
The black shoelaces talked
to him in his sleep, the poems
drifting beyond the man's bed
to recite themselves into being.

Jacob's black shoes glistened
as if they were shined yesterday,
the sleepy man looking over
the edge of his bed as the talking
shoes tapped a message that said
a man who wears someone else's
shoes is a man who knows how
to get along in life. When he put
them on at dawn, the shoes quit
reciting poetry and led the man
to a church Jacob never entered.

The new owner of the shoes went
into a church for the first time
in thirty years, the shoes echoing
across the sanctuary where a priest
waited, sensing Jewish shoes.
After the stranger revealed his sins
to the priest, he emerged from
the confessional and looked down

at his bare feet. He went back to
the tiny chamber, but Jacob's shoes
were gone, their disappearance casting
 a steady light on the barefoot
man, the helpless priest, even
the two mice in the sanctuary that
revealed themselves to no one as
they gnawed on the twisted shoelaces.

The Third Miracle

Casting, flaying, assuming and folding,
he wears the stories of conquest on
his neck, cuts and bruises healing
to give him the courage to get out
coughing, shaking and mistaking
the curtain of treasures as his own—
the two headed doll bleeding on
the necklace, the healing sticks
and the exploding blossoms, dried
roses coming to life on his chest,
adjusting to the turtle claws tied
there, stiff spiders fossilized in his hair
as he leans forward to enter the rocks,
the taunting tails of iguanas choking him,
weighing him down, keeping him close
to the ground where water seeps and
drinks him heaving, jolting, resisting,
covering his blue body with the foam
of riches, earth murmurs tugging at
the string of snake rattles, broken
mirrors, balls of poison from a Gila
monster, the objects tied to his heart
to keep him digging and groping,
sending his legs under the heavy
rock to pin him and make him
a figure someone will dig up one
day, shocked the living man is
displaying what vanished when
the dust storm never ended but
turned white, its clouds covering
the world because what hung on
his neck, underground, never died.
It revolved around his infinite heart.

The Owl

The owl in the trees doesn't move,
its claws embedded in the branch.

There is heavy traffic across the river
where I have watched drug dealers drown.

When Pancho Villa was shot, children stood
by his bullet-riddled car and stared.

I love the magnolia tree, its golden leaves
videotaped for an unreleased movie

about the end of the world.
I keep a secret no one wants, been afraid

of the dark, but the basket of bootleg Dylan
tapes was sold to the highest bidder in 1975.

The owl is a statue thrown in the trees
by an escaped convict who made it to Mexico.

The wings are hollow and full of cocaine,
but the dealer is dead.

The last hooting of an owl I heard was in 1932,
when my grandfather worked the Arizona railroads

in 112-degree heat, clearing the desert of owls
with a hammer, spikes, and a drink of water or two.

Murmur

Spider web combed in time.
Constant blossom.
Listen.

Horn of fire, mouth of stars.
Belt worn to fend off the storm.
Two ways of entering the mountain.

Murmur of clouds, frame of the river.
Burned sticks in a circle.
Footprint talk, sore wrist.
Long rain and equation.
Necklaces are scars.

Angel thought, guitar arrival.
Wing dream.
Snow capped peaks past belief.

Buried in the rocks—council eye
spinning the ring of the moon.
Kneeling between oceans.
The tossed wheel is a blue
forehead opening its eyes.

Predator leaves thumbnail behind.
Names the horizon without a name.
Word tongues the crows.
Snowflake cry.
Name it.

Somewhere North of Las Cruces

The night desert is not afraid.
Lights in the distance surround
what took place centuries ago.
To imagine the dark landscape
is to laugh and wake the dead.
Roads point north, turn south
when mountains shroud the canyons,
their black shapes resembling Maria
Madresca and Juana Salinas making
the sign of the cross on their foreheads.

The highway disappears near the river
where an old man used to be afraid,
his sacrifice leaving two dogs, one
horse, and several wild birds.
When the 110 degree heat came,
he went away, walking to the sun.
When the river dried, the road
stopped at the shrine.

The night desert hides an oath
to the land that remains.
No one stops here and no one
understands why the flowers
and statues are overgrown in weeds,
the altar glowing below the black
sky where the old man saw
something he couldn't name.

Keep

I kept dreaming and finally sat up
in bed, the morning smelling like

a stone lion, its silence intact,
my breathing coming back as

I blinked and realized I was no
longer afraid, though the body

lying on the beach had tail feathers
and the head of an ancient priest

who told me the teacher who dreams
is the sleeper left behind by the dream.

The Flat Desert

The flat desert spills red out
of the falling sun.

Three men cross and
three men go back.

When they pause to pray,
the dust storm begins.

When they think they see
a tall crucifix on a distant

sand dune, the brown
cloud ends.

The flat desert enters
the whole of the earth,

not the perceived
soul of God, but

the vessel where
travelers are safe.

The flat desert drinks
from the canyon where

a river flows, becoming
the hot terrain that doesn't

accept men, the three
crossing again, looking

for a way out of
sacred landscapes.

Your Hands

Your scars are fine.
They touch the border wall
with humility that carries
your soul to the other side.

The man who feels the fear
in his hands is the boy
who gets wet each time
he runs his fingers over
the trunk of the tree.

Your hands are afraid
to welcome him because
the morning sends the cooing
dove away.
You are late for the meal and
there is someone waiting
to love you.

Save Twilight

The book cover is a
photograph of Julio Cortázar

and his cat, Theodore Adorno.
It looks like my beloved Lucy

that died recently, my spirit
animal I found long ago,

Lucy sleeping next to me,
even in death, because I still

feel her claws on the mattress,
her weight against my back.

Cortázar smiles at Adorno,
pointing with his hand,

the cat reaching out with a paw
to bless the writer that knows

a cat is a tiny God sent down
to make sure every word is there.

He Calls His Dog Rimbaud

after Charles Simic

The sausages have been sliced.
The wine has grown old.
The piano notes belong to the man
lifting his hands from brushing
Rimbaud, his dog. Women have left him.

One or two poems belong in the books.
He has a gift for knowing what people do.
He was cited as the one who found the image
hidden inside the caves of the emperor.

When he writes, his dog howls and gives him
ideas to take on the boat.
The hat and boots have been laid out.
The perfumed photo of the woman has been torn.

The piano notes settle in the soul of
the quiet man hugging his pet and
asking for a growl.
He will meet the light on the next continent,

walk toward it because everyone wants him
to explain why other dogs ran away.
He is driven to get to the nature of this dog.
He must find why the paws trouble his sleep,

why he has to leave in order to speak and try
to imitate the dumb dog by barking at
nothing in the street, must find why
the wagging tongue of the animal hangs
so far out of its mouth, so he calls out,
"Rimbaud! Come here, boy!"

Rufino Tamayo

In "El Quemado," the burned one raises his flaming
arms to the dark sky, the painting swirling in smoke
and the fumes given to branding dimensions with fire.
The figure runs, his hair aflame, brown legs changing
history by surviving the bridge to the other side.

"Hombre en rojo" allows the red man to emerge with
swollen cheeks, his crimson skin reflecting the battle
where his mother and father were taken in red, the skull
of el hombre glowing red with incident, open mouth
releasing a red and white bubble, the red man's life
given to turning his head to the left where the red river
flows and never stops approaching.

"El iluminado" is in the cosmos, his bare white head
glowing among the stars and constellations that misspell
his name because comets bouncing off his shoulders
carry a different story across the universe, his naked
brown body exposing an enormous penis that hangs
there, pointing underground because his limp left arm
won't touch it and his right one rests across his belly,
meteors pelting him with thought, granting him
permission to be the one to step forward.

Three "Hombres en el espacio" hurl beyond space,
arms open as if three crucifixions are taking place,
each man resembling a jet plane that rose too far,
bodies becoming metallic missiles that reinvent
color each time they wander beyond what Tamayo
intended, his trio joining the sun as they reach apogee,
vanish with arms extended in the jubilation of the cross,

though el "Hombre confrontando al infinito" appears
beyond the pink scratched sun he contemplates, skies
empty of stars, the silhouetted figure a keyhole Tamayo
opened into infinity and gave the silhouetted man
time to hide his face because the painter welcomed
his hombres without giving them names.

Invisible

The stone stairs down to the cellar
are a way out of the story,
its beating music left behind by
startled pigeons that survived
the smoke in the cathedral,
the blinding sun in the Juárez plaza
sending you across the bridge, the red
glare of noon swallowing forgiveness.
The playground was lit in bright sun
and sweat, the boys hitting the ball
until it was your turn and you hit
the only home run in your life, driving
in three runs and winning the game.
They ignored you after that because
the Mexican on the team was not
supposed to round the bases,
but strike out instead.

The border was rained on for years.
Your brother wasn't there, stepping
through mud because it is for
the oldest son missing from the city.
What this brings is caked designs
on muddy hands darker than
an absent father, the rain pounding
the roof as if he wanted to get in.
The border was invisible for years.
Your family was there being
painted on city walls.
When your ancestors rose from
the dead, the border opened its
barriers and everyone entered.
What this has to do with you can
be found on the glowing letters
spray painted on the walls.
When you were middle-aged,
they carved puppets to honor you.

The Fourth Miracle

He rises out of the adobe walls,
hair on fire, empty sun and knotted
hands, dust spelling an alphabet
in the air, choking him at birth,
trapping him in the structure that
germs the walls with signs and windows,
mounting the mud to change the world.
He crashes out of the adobe layers to
frighten the myth and deposit dirt
inside the exploding heart of timbers,
the crash splintering a known thing
not witnessed because everyone
fled before he came out of the walls.
He elevates beyond the roof,
the holes there teasing the light with
disintegrating brick, fire of sand
splashing clouds that cover his
stepping forth as an unexpected
act in capturing the town.

He emerges from hidden sin,
the act of being pasted to the wall
forgiven, though his brown arms
and legs burn with the suffocating
wind of wanting to be marked and
slammed against the door to fall
through an implosion sending
the house to hell.
He ascends through the order of bricks,
realigns the breath of angels to resemble
the work of women sweeping what must
stay clean for the next son to be born.
He breaks both hands coming out,
the grip of the prisoner becoming
the fists of the wanted and the skill

of the builder, the underground
creator shifting foundations to drop
adobe layers upon his dead, giving
him dirt to dream it is only a house
and not the weight of home.

Hollow Ground

The pots of frozen plants outside,
a gray sky ignored for something
that moves in difficult patterns
as I wonder where my father went.
I call my mother who lives alone
and my sister answers, tells me
she is sleeping and everything is okay.
I want to believe it but the years
of staying away have changed the
road across the desert and I remain,
tracing images of duration as long
as I can, the people on the other side
of memory coming and going, lying
down and lying to their children.

Once, as a boy, I saw a large desert
turtle cross the dirt road and I paused,
watched it take forever to move,
its huge head dusty and brown,
the enormous shell covered with
intricate symbols that told me
I was standing on the wrong earth.
I should have been over there,
where the voices in the mountain
announce the turtle is welcome,
the slow creature given a place
to remove the weight off its back.

The Poet at the Tree

When Robert Burlingame, my teacher,
dwelled at the tree, the cottonwood
fought lightning until he folded his hands.
When he emerged from its limbs
with pigeon droppings on his boots,
it was justice for men who need
to walk far from home,
away from the unreliable river
and the pueblo hidden from view.
When Robert recited at the stone gate,
I learned you must speak when
the cholla bleeds for you.

I listened to the prickly pear rip thorns
for Robert's lines about flowers,
lost arroyos, and the wounded owl.
They became words about the woman
he left in Las Cruces when it thundered.
Robert vanished under the branches,
his voice hidden in the tree.
I fought against nothing, yearned for
the cottonwood that stood for
our names—ages of veins that were
touched gently by the falling leaves
when he died.

Beautiful

Thinking of the beautiful flame
on the fingertips of a young man

who fought for freedom.
Must be heaven hanging there,

his mother cried.
Must be a dream where no one

was killed, the old men
wished as they sat back.

Thinking of the lovely way
the fingers fold around the flower.

Must be the thrush setting up
its school in the tree,

no one pronounced.
Must be the way we go home,

the angels decided before
letting it rain.

Balata

It was peaceful and I wanted
to be lost in a holy town,

but the wars were dying down,
casualty lists posted on the other

side of Mars, the earth beyond saving
because the soil sprouted blue

and orange veins that gave life
to what I couldn't reach.

I found a beautiful river in one
daydream where my dead nephew

did not go to war and I was
an old man who knew nothing,

my chalkboard filled with equations
the ants carried across the soil, a line

of them climbing through the vapor
of a god that took what he wanted

as those who nodded off in my
daydream woke up and saved me.

Soul Over Lightning

Let us imagine our hands reach
beyond the desk and lamp,
cold fingers tracing the story of
the great shapes as they turn into
fields of sunflowers where the song
the migrant sings is the shadow
in yellow recognition of who we are.
When each step into the cathedral
is announced, there is no staircase
to inhabit the divine, this pause
offering a chance to release what
loves us and demands it in return.

Let us carry our dead in our pockets
and toss their seeds at the earth,
placing faith in the breath of poverty—
sound of recognition where no one
answers and the streets are housed
in the anecdote of light.
When we pray to dirt floors, rooms
come alive, their passage into the past
blocked by white mountains seeking
a voice that is believable when roots
of trees end in rock strewn solitude
and we lie to the rain and lie inside it.

About the Author

Ray Gonzalez is a professor in the English Department at the University of Minnesota, Twin Cities. He is the author of ten books of poetry, including *Faith Run* (University of Arizona Press, 2009); *Cool Auditor: Prose Poems* (BOA Editions, 2009); *Consideration of the Guitar* (BOA Editions, 2005); *The Religion of Hands* (University of Arizona Press, 2005), which received the 2006 Latino Heritage Award for Best Book of Poetry; *The Hawk Temple at Tierra Grande* (BOA Editions, 2002), the winner of a 2003 Minnesota Book Award; *Turtle Pictures* (University of Arizona Press, 2000), the winner of a 2001 Minnesota Book Award; and *The Heat of Arrivals* (BOA Editions, 1996), the winner of a 1997 PEN/Josephine Miles Book Award. He is the author of three books of nonfiction: *Renaming the Earth: Personal Essays* (University of Arizona Press, 2008); *Memory Fever* (University of Arizona Press, 1999); and *The Underground Heart* (University of Arizona Press, 2002), which received the 2003 Carr P. Collins/Texas Institute of Letters Award for Best Book of Nonfiction. He is also the author of two books of short stories: *The Ghost of John Wayne* (University of Arizona Press, 2001) and *Circling the Tortilla Dragon* (Creative Art Books, 2002). His poetry has appeared in the 1999, 2000, 2003, and 2014 editions of *The Best American Poetry*. He is the editor of twelve anthologies, including *Sudden Fiction Latino: Short Short Fiction from the U.S. and Latin America* (W. W. Norton, 2010) and *No Boundaries: Prose Poems by 24 Poets* (Tupelo Press, 2002). He has served as poetry editor of *The Bloomsbury Review* since 1980, and he received a Lifetime Achievement Award in Literature from the Border Regional Library Association in 2003.

Soul Over Lightning

Camino del Sol
A Latina and Latino Literary Series